No Stress No Hassel

Navern Nelson

ISBN: 978-1-949343-87-8

DEDICATION

I dedicated this book to my everlasting Father,
God Almighty. In Him I live, breathe, move and
have my being.

ACKNOWLEDGMENT

I use this opportunity to thank my wife, Jinel Nelson, for her constant love and support as I wrote this book.

Thanks to my grandmother, Mama Madeline, who instilled values in me and who kept believing in me that I could complete this and other books. She was my source of inspiration to write a book.

Big up to mi brethren, Sandrass, who kept me motivated throughout this entire process.

Thanks to Aunt Edith who always had me in her prayers and kept me on track spiritually.

Thanks to Melicia Mathison, who was instrumental in making this book a reality.

TABLE OF CONTENTS

WHEN YOUR STRENGTH IS GONE

When your strength is gone

Remember, God is mighty and strong

He will never let you go

You keep holding on to His unchanging hands

And remember This:

"NO weapon formed against you shall prosper"

SOMETIMES WE ARE TESTED

Sometimes we are tested not to expose our

weakness,

But to discover our strengths.

Don't stress about the closed doors behind you

New doors, God is opening for you,

Just keep moving forward.

DON'T FOCUS ON WHO DARKENED YOUR DAYS

Don't focus on who darkened your days

Appreciate who brightened them

Don't focus on who let you down

Appreciate who lifted you up

Don't focus on yesterday,

Yesterday is behind,

The future is not yet

It is what you do now that matters

JAH KNOW

Jah Know

God promises there is something better ahead

We can't always see where the road leads,

But we just have to trust Him.

Rest in Him.

My God is powerful and mighty.

TODay

Today

May the Lord strengthen your mind, body and
spirit.

When you're weary, may you be refreshed.

When you're exhausted and worn out, may you be
renewed.

When you're broken, may you be restored.

When you're afraid, may you become
courageous and strong.

Walk in complete confidence and faith knowing
that Almighty God is with you every step of
your journey. Bless up.

DEAR GOD

Dear God

I bring my burdens to You.

You know my situation

You know I can't make it without You

Comfort my heart,

Give me strength and

Help me carry on, in Jesus Christ name.

Thank You, *Abba* Father.

"I AM" THE GOD OF MOSES

"I Am" the God of Moses

If He could close the lion's mouth for Daniel,

Part the Red Sea for Moses,

Make the sun stand still for Joshua,

Make David slay Goliath with a sling and a stone,

Make Samson slay over 1,000 Philistines with a

      donkey jawbone...

Stay in faith

God opened the prison doors for Peter,

Put a baby in Sarah's arm,

Raise Lazarus from the dead.

He can certainly take care of you.

23

Fact

Fact:

The same God who made a way the last time

Will make a way this time and forever.

Selah.

Hallelujah!!

Facts

Drink from the fountain of ABBA,

And you will never thirst again.

Hallelujah.

Selah.

Yashua, Jesus Christ of Nazareth is the Fountain of

Life

NOTHING IN NATURE LIVES OF ITSELF

Nothing in nature lives of itself

Rivers don't drink their own water,

It runs to the sea.

Trees don't eat their own fruits.

The moon, stars and sun doesn't shine for itself.

A flower's fragrance is not for itself.

YAHWAH is the Ruler of us all.

Living for each other is the Rule of Nature.

ONLY JAH CAN TURN

Only Jah can turn

A mess into a message

A test into a testimony

A trial into a triumph

A victim into a victor

Only Jah is good,

All the time.

MaY ABBA FATHER

May ABBA FATHER

Strengthen your mind, body and spirit.

When you're weary, may you be refreshed.

When you're exhausted and worn out, may you be

renewed.

When you're broken, may you be restored.

When you're afraid, may you become courageous

and strong.

Walk in complete confidence and faith

Knowing that ABBA FATHER, God Almighty,

Is with you every step of the way. Selah.

AN ARROW

An arrow can only be shot by pulling it backward.

When life is dragging you back with difficulties,

Just imagine that it's going to launch you into

      something great.

Hallelujah.

GOOD MORNING

Good Morning

Morning is a wonderful blessing given by God.

It may be cloudy or sunny,

But it is an unwrapped gift;

A gift that gives us another start

To what we define as life.

I pray you wake up

Feeling thankful, hopeful, loved and blessed.

GOD WILL

God will never leave you empty.

He will replace everything you lost.

If He ask you to put something down,

It's because He wants you to pick up something

greater.

What habit will you put down?

POWER AND MONEY

Power and money are fruits of life!

But family and friends are roots of life.

We can manage without fruits

But we can never stand without "Roots."

CONFIDENCE

We plan big things for tomorrow

In spite of zero knowledge of the future

Or having any certainty of uncertainties.

Every Word of God is pure,

He is a shield unto them

Who put their trust in Him.

Bless up.

A BEAUTIFUL LIFE

A beautiful life does not just happen.

It's built daily with:

Love,

Laughter,

Sacrifice,

Patience,

Grace and Forgiveness.

Life is beautiful, enjoy it.

MaY JaH

May Jah provide you with your daily need,

Keep you warm and comfortable,

Keep you safe with peace and love.

Much love and blessings.

AS THE SKY

As the sky breaks into a beautiful sunrise,

May God open heaven's door to shower you

With lots of love and happiness

To make your day a meaningful one.

God bless.

ABBA FATHER, YAHSHUA

Abba Father, Yahshua, Jesus Christ.

When you kneel before the Father and the Son,

They will stand up for you.

When He stands up for you,

No one can stand against you.

Hallelujah.

THERE ARE TIMES

There are times when prayer is the only gift

We can give to the ones we care for.

So I pray to God the Father,

To make you happy and guide you safely.

Grant you wealth, give you good health and,

Most of all, answer your prayers.

NEVER

Never think hard about the past,

It brings tears.

Don't think more about the future,

It brings fear.

Live this moment with a smile,

It brings cheers.

MAN'S STEPS

Man's steps are ordained by the Lord,

How then can man understand his way?

See Proverbs 20:24.

MAY GOD GO

May God go before you today

And make a way where there seems to be no way.

May He place the right people in your path and

    more,

And move the wrong people out of the way.

Amen.

Have a blessed day.

GIVE GOD

Give God

Your

Weaknesses and

He

Will give you

His strength.

TODAY IS

Today is a beautiful day.

May Jah,

Grant you good health, lasting comfort

And relief from the burdens of life;

Bless your heart with love and faith;

Comfort your soul with gladness and inner peace;

And touch your life with contentment.

May Jah take care of all your needs.

MY PRAYER FOR YOU

May God fill your life with purpose,

Days with wonderful memories,

Heart with love and peace,

Mind with wisdom and discernment,

Soul with praise and thanksgiving,

Body with vibrant health,

Friends with loyalty and trust,

Family with unity and joy.

Prayer is the most important conversation of the

day.

Take it to God before you take it to anyone else.

FAITH

Just believe, you are going to make it.

You and your family will be just fine.

"Just stand and let Me fight this battle,"

Says the Lord God Almighty.

Selah.

MAY THE LORD

May the Lord grant you what you hope for.

Reward you with what you work for.

Bless you with what you pray for.

And, most of all, surprise you with what you have

   not asked for.

Because, all the time, God is truly good.

YOU

You sit still and trust the engineer when a train

goes through a tunnel and it gets dark,

You don't throw away the ticket and jump off.

You just trust God, no matter how dark your

situation is.

God says, "You are coming out victorious!"

OPEN YOUR EYES

Open your eyes to a beautiful day.

Appreciate where you are in your journey,

Even if it is not where you want to be.

Every season serves a purpose.

THERE IS

There is one today,

Between the thousands of yesterdays

And countless tomorrows.

How can I let it pass without saying,

"I Love You."

GOD SAYS

God says,

"Those who hope in Me will not be disappointed."

See Isaiah 49:23.

HaVE A LOVELY DaY

Have a lovely day

The most useful asset of a person is not

A head full of knowledge

But a heart full of love,

With ears open to listen,

And hands willing to help each other.

SOMEONE

Someone asked a saint, "What is anger?"

He gave a beautiful answer:

"It is a punishment we give to ourselves

for somebody else's mistake."

GIVE MUCH

Give much and expect little from others,

Keep your heart free from hate

And your mind free from worry.

Live simple and fill your life with love.

Treasure your family and friends.

Treat others how you expect to be treated.

This is the key to happiness.

"I AM"

"I Am" ABBA Father.

Jesus opens the day with

Grace, success, protection and blessings for you.

As flowers open every morning with sweet scents,

So does the hand of God.

MaY THE LORD

May the Lord

Release His anointing oil upon your head now

Today, in Jesus' name.

Receive it.

Hallelujah.

HEALTH

Health does not always come from medicines.

Most of the time, it comes from peace of mind,

Peace in the heart and soul.

It comes from laughter and love.

NOW

Now I am smiling because the Lord gave me the

privilege to see the light of the day!

Another day of unbelievable breakthroughs,

Another chance to do the best in my life.

Another moment to say "Thank You" to the most

Beloved Jah.

Thank You for another day to be alive and well.

SOMEONE CARES

Someone cares

Someone remembers your name.

Your name is whispered in someone's prayers.

Keep this beautiful feeling in mind:

Someone is always wishing good for you.

Have a wonderful day.

GOOD DAY!

Good Day!

Let the light of the day rise in your heart

To fill your day with

Love, joy, blessings and protection from God.

TRUST IN GOD

Trust in God

You will never be lost.

Wait for God,

No time is lost.

Walk with God,

No strength is lost.

Talk with God,

No breath is lost.

Selah.

A Day

A day full of joyful moments I am wishing you.

The most powerful weapon against trials;

The most effective medicine against sickness, and

The most valuable gift to someone

is SINCERE PRAYER.

Selah.

GOD IS

God is Good!

Rise and shine!

He is in control of all things!

Believe!

Stay blessed! and

Have a blessed day today.

YOU ARE

You are a child of the Most High God.

You are amazing.

You are worthy.

Your best days are still ahead of you.

You can do all things though Christ Jesus.

No weapon will prosper against you.

No enemy will defeat you.

God is working everything in your favour,

In *YAHSHUA,* JESUS CHRIST'S HOLY NAME.

THERE ARE TIMES

There are times when prayer is the only gift

We can give to the ones we care for.

So I prayed to God to make you happy,

Guide you safely and grant you wealth.

Give you good health and,

Most of all, answer all your prayers.

THE KEY

The key to happiness is to be able

To change pain into pleasure,

Darkness into light and

Sorrow into joy.

This can occur only if

We have the courage to change.

BE ENCOURAGED

Be encouraged today.

When God, MOST HIGH YAHWEH,

Starts something, He finishes it.

Be confident!

He won't give up on you.

He will complete the work He began in you.

Amen.

Selah.

A FaTHER

A Father said to his son,

"Be careful where you walk."

The son responded,

"You be careful. Remember, I am following in

 your footsteps."

LIFE IS

Life is about balance!

Be kind but don't let people abuse you.

Trust but don't be deceived.

Be content, but never stop improving yourself.

STRENGTH

Strength doesn't come from what you can do.

It comes from overcoming the things

You once thought you couldn't.

ANOTHER NEW DAY

Another new day

One more, new step

One more, new hope

If you don't leave your past in the past

It will destroy your future.

Live for what today has to offer,

Not what yesterday has taken away.

Successful days ahead.

YOUR MIND

Your mind is a powerful thing.

When you fill it with positive thoughts,

Your life will start to change.

Jah

Jah is our perfect Guide in life.

His strength overcomes our weaknesses.

His grace fills our emptiness.

His presence overcomes our loneliness.

Walk with Jah every day and

Never underestimate the power of your prayers.

Jah Bless You.

HAVE A GREAT DAY

Have a great day

May this day bring you

More blessings and less challenges.

May you feel loved and love others.

May you feel the sun on your face and smile.

Wishing you a day full of

Sunny smiles and happy thoughts!

EXODUS 12!

Happy New Year!

We made it through another year.

Thank You, Lord.

ABBA Father.

LIFE CAN BE

Life can be full of unexpected things,

Either happy or sad.

No matter what may happen,

Always keep a loving heart,

A wise mind and a strong faith in God

Who will always stay with us

Throughout the journey of our life.

Keep the faith.

Bless.

YOU NEVER KNOW

You never know how strong you are

Until being strong is your only choice.

JAH BLESS.

WE NEED

We need at least four basic elements to survive:

1. Water
2. Air
3. Food
4. Light

We need Jesus Christ, Yeshua, to live.

Look what the Bible tells us about Jesus Christ,

Yeshua:

1. I am the Living Water.
2. I am the Breath of Life.
3. I am the Bread of Life.
4. I am the Light of the World.

What do you think?

ABBA FATHER IS

ABBA Father is faithful.

Having ABBA Father in your boat

Doesn't mean you'll not face any storm.

But it means that no storm can sink your boat!

Walk in faith and you'll never walk alone.

Be blessed.

AND JESUS SAID

And Jesus said to him, "If you can believe,

All things are possible for the one who

believes."

See Mark 9:23.

GOD ARMS

God arms me with strength and

He makes my way perfect.

See Psalm 18:32.

Dear Lord God,

Thank You for the strength You bless me with.

I need You.

I trust that all will work out,

According to Your perfect plan.

Selah.

FOR THIS

For this light momentary affliction is preparing for

us an eternal weight of glory beyond all

comparison.

As we look not to the things that are seen but to

the things that are unseen.

For the things that are seen are transient, but the

things that are unseen are eternal.

See 2 Corinthians 4:17-18.

WHATEVER

Whatever life throws at you,

Even if it hurts you,

Just be strong and fight through it.

Remember, strong walls shake

But never collapse.

DEAR LORD

Dear Lord, Yes, You are my Rock and my Shelter,

In Your arms I am safe and secure.

Please protect me and my loved ones this day.

Selah.

WE MaKE

We make mistakes,

We erase, but we become better as we are

     sharpened.

We are like pencils,

The best part of us is inside.

We make a mark as we touch others' lives.

Pages of yesterday cannot be revised,

But the pages of today and tomorrow are blank.

You hold the pencil so make your mark.

DEAR GOD

Dear God, Good Father,

Thank You for the gift of family and friends.

I pray that You embrace these wonderful people

In my life with Your loving arms.

Keep them safe and happy.

Shower them with all the blessings they need.

MAY GOD GO BEFORE YOU

May God go before You this weekend and

Make the rough roads smooth.

May His joy be your strength and

May His peace fill your heart today and always.

Have a beautiful weekend in Jesus' Name.

IN THE NAME OF YAHWEH

In the Name of YAHWEH, ABBA FATHER.

What you have, many can have.

What you are, no one can be.

Knowledge will give you power,

But character will give you respect.

Amen.

THaNK YOU GOD

Thank You, God, for this beautiful day.

Guide my feet in the way I should go.

Make me a better person.

I thank You for Your presence in my life every

day.

Amen.

STRENGTH FOR TODAY

The Lord is the strength of my life,

Of whom shall I be afraid.

See Psalm 27:1.

Give me strength for today Lord, wherever I go.

Let no danger daunt me, whatever the foe.

Let no task o'ercome me.

No trial, my heart fret

I would walk with Thee, Lord,

In the path Thou hast set

Let no burden o'ercome me.

Give me strength to bear.

Then I shall have courage, whatever my care.

Let no grief o'erwhelm me, wherever I am.

Give me strength.

THE JOY OF LIFE

The joy of life comes

From the wisdom of counting your blessings,

Never your troubles.

Focus on what you have,

And maintain a good thankful heart.

TODAY'S BLESSING

We are all blessed again today with the gift of life.

Thank God and let's make something good today.

Help others who need it.

Think of others who are less fortunate.

One small positive thought in the morning

Can change your whole day.

PRAYER

ABBA Father, thank You for a new day.

Thank You for leading, guiding, and directing us.

Thank You for showing us Your way.

ABBA Father, help us to live our lives in You

and for You.

We need You, we love You, we exalt You, and we

praise You.

ABBA Father, we ask that You go before us to

make all our crooked place straight, in

Jesus name.

Amen.

Selah.

SEE HOW

See how beautifully

God has added one more day to your life,

Not necessarily because you need it,

But because someone else needs "YOU."

Be blessed.

DEAR LORD GOD

Dear Lord God,

Grant me courage as I go through this day.

When I am tempted to give up,

Help me to keep going.

Grant me a cheerful spirit

When things don't go my way, and

Give me courage

To do whatever needs to be done.

In Jesus' name.

Amen.

Selah.

YOU ARE HIGHLY FAVOURED

You are highly favoured.

Love makes all things easy.

Faith makes all things possible.

Hope makes all things work.

Have a glorious day.

THERE IS

There is no door God's mercy cannot open.

It opened Bartimaeus' blind eyes;

It opened Elisabeth's barren womb;

It opened the Red Sea and

Terminated 430 years of slavery.

Therefore, I pray for you today that every

good door shut against your life shall be

opened by the mercy of God, in the mighty

name of Jesus Christ of Nazareth.

SOME PEOPLE

Some people aren't really loyal.

They only pretend to be for an opportunity or

If they need you for some reason.

They will continue to play loyal until a better

opportunity arises or they no longer need you,

then that is where their loyalty will end.

WHEN YOU CaRRY A BIBLE

When you carry a Bible

The devil gets a headache.

When you open it, he collapses.

When he sees you reading it, he faints.

When he sees you living it, he flees.

Now you are going to get two copies of this book

    and "SHARE."

He will try to discourage you.

I just defeated him.

Get one more copy and share now, in Jesus' name.

Amen. Selah.

DEUTERONOMY 28:7

Deuteronomy 28:7

As your enemies gather to plan your downfall and

setbacks,

God shall confuse and dismiss them in seven

directions.

You shall be blessed seven times more,

Until the blessed can call you blessed.

Just believe and it is so, in Jesus' name.

Selah.

A PRAYER

A Prayer for the coming week.

Dear Lord, prepare me for the coming week.

Take away my worries and regrets.

Recharge my soul and renew my hope.

Please go before me,

Clear the way and protect me.

Bring the right people into my life and

Move the wrong people out of the way.

Guide me with your love and give me your joy,

In Jesus' mighty Name I pray.

Amen.

MAY GOD BLESS

May God bless you:

Spiritually

Physically,

Emotionally and

Financially.

Today and always.

Have a good day.

BE LIKE A TREE

Be like a tree - stay grounded.

Connect with your roots,

Turn over a new leaf.

Bend before you break,

Enjoy your unique natural beauty.

Keep growing.

THE GOD WE SERVE

The God we serve

Is able to deliver.

See Daniel 3:17.

Lord, thank You for being with us,

No matter what we are going through.

MaY GOD BE ABOVE YOU

May God be:

Above you - to bless you;

Below you - to support you;

Before you - to guide you;

Behind you - to protect you;

Beside you - to comfort you;

Inside you - to give you strength and joy.

Amen.

TRAIN YOUR MIND

Train your mind to see the good in everything.

Positivity is a choice.

The happiness of your life

Depends on the quality of your thoughts.

Everyday holds the possibility of a miracle.

Have a nice day.

THE HaPPINESS

The happiness of your life

Depends upon the quality of your thoughts.

So, think happy and positive and so it is.

LIFE IS

Life is like music,

It has high notes and low notes.

No matter how high or low your notes may be,

Keep in tune with God and

You will never go out of tune in the music of life.

IT'S AMAZING

It's amazing that living in simplicity

Gives true contentment,

We go as we come into this world.

In the end, nothing is ours to keep.

So, let's share what we have:

Smiles, hugs, God's Word,

Time, friendship and love.

Love more, hate less,

Ignore critics and enjoy life.

Life is so short and

Too precious to waste it on worries.

SEE

See what great love

ABBA FATHER has lavished on us,

That we should be called Children of God;

And that is who we are!

See 1 John 3:1.

MAY THE HOLY WEEKEND

May the holy weekend

Burst forth in the joy of

Resurrected life for you and your loved ones,

On the blessed Sabbath.

TOMORROW

Tomorrow is never promised,

So today, I want all my friends and family

to know how thankful I am that all of you are in

my life.

God bless.

JOY

Joy and praise on Sunday.

Prayer on Monday.

Peace on Tuesday.

God's favour on Wednesday.

A thankful heart on Thursday.

Remembrance on Friday.

God's comfort on Saturday.

Add it all up.

May the Spirit of God bring you

New blessings always, in Jesus' name.

IT IS

It is not created by the shoes we wear,

But by the steps we take.

Let's make our journey of life

Meaningful and memorable.

Good day.

Bless up.

THANK YOU

Thank You heavenly Father

For today's early morning rising.

May I see the world today,

Through the divine lens of your eyes, Lord.

May I align with Your will for my life, in Jesus

Name.

Dear Father,

May I also be lost in Your glorious presence and

shine a light of love upon everyone, in

the name of Jesus Christ I pray.

Amen.

Selah.

MORNING PRAYER

Thank you, Lord,

For blessing me to see this beautiful day.

Oh Lord, this morning,

I pray that You keep my family and friends safe

From all distress and pain.

Lord, please be by my side and guide my steps in

Every way, in Your name I pray.

Amen.

Selah.

IT'S THE START OF A NEW DAY

It's the start of a new day.

May love surround you,

Joy walk with you,

Laughter sing with you,

Success guide you,

And good health bless you.

Have a blessed and wonderful day,

In the name of Jesus.

BE BLESSED

Be Blessed

Remember how blessed you are to see another

day.

Enjoy it.

Not everyone has that privilege.

Jah bless.

Selah.

WHAT GOD IS ABOUT TO DO

What God is about to do

In your life is going to

Cause people to want to know the God you serve.

Keep believing and expect the best.

I AM

I Am ABBA Father.

May love and laughter light your heart and home.

May good and faithful friends be yours wherever

you may roam.

May peace and plenty bless your world with joy

that long endures.

May all life's passing seasons bring the best to

you and yours.

NOTHING

Nothing feels better

Than knowing that God loves me,

That He will always be there for me,

And that He will always take care of me.

Jah know.

MAY GOD

May God be above you to always bless you,

Below you to protect you,

Before you to guide you,

Behind you to protect you,

Beside you to comfort you,

And most of all

To be inside you to give you strength and

joy.

Amen.

Selah.

FAITH

Faith makes all things possible.

Love makes everything beautiful.

Hope makes all things work.

May you have an abundance of all three and

more.

Every day, may there always be peace in your

heart and love and laughter in your home.

Be blessed.

FORGET

Forget the things that made you sad,

Remember those that made you glad.

Forget the trouble that passed away,

Remember the blessings that come each day.

DEAR GOD

Dear God, I know that I'm not perfect.

I know sometimes I forget to pray.

I know sometimes I lose my temper,

But thank You for loving me unconditionally,

And giving me another day to start over.

Amen.

Selah.

I AM

I am blessed,

I am not lucky.

Everything I have is because of

Jah's grace and favour for me.

Jah is

Jah is going to give me

More than I am asking for

Because He loves me,

And I believe it with all

My heart, mind and soul.

Hallelujah.

Selah.

A MORNING PRAYER

Almighty God,

Take my hands and lead me through this day.

Step by step, remind me that I cannot do

Everything I wish, nor do any of it perfectly.

Only You are perfect.

Only with Your help can I do my best.

Help me to remember to ask for that help.

Selah.

I AM THE GOD OF MOSES

The God of our father ABRAHAM.

Bless this home with the overflowing of LOVE,

With the overflowing of LOYALTY,

With the overflowing of FORGIVENESS,

With the overflowing of GOOD FRIENDSHIPS,

With the overflowing of HOPE,

With the overflowing of TENDERNESS,

With the overflowing of FAITH,

With the overflowing of LAUGHTER.

Take love and loyalty, mix it thoroughly with faith.

Blend it with tenderness, kindness,

understanding, friendship and hope.

Sprinkle abundantly with laughter. Bake it with sunshine. Serve daily with a generous helping.

This is a happy home recipe.

A PRAYER

A Prayer for a special child, yes you and me.

Lord God,

Surround this child with goodness and mercy.

Lead them in Your light each day.

Let them walk the path You have chosen for them.

Guide their steps along the way.

Teach them to trust Your wisdom

And obey Your loving plans for them.

Keep them from all harm,

Protect them as they go along life's road,

In Yahshua, Jesus Christ holy name. Amen.

LORD JESUS CHRIST

Lord Jesus Christ,

Help us to remember when we first met,

And the strong love that grew between us.

Help us love in practical ways so nothing can

divide us.

May our words be kind and our thoughts gracious.

May we remain gracious and humble enough to

ask for forgiveness,

And wise enough to freely give.

REMEMBER

Remember the blessing that come each day.

Forget the things that made you sad and

Remember those that made you glad.

Forget the troubles that passed away.

Tell someone you love them today.

You have to stop worrying, wondering and

     doubting.

Have faith that things will work out IN JESUS

     NAME.

Amen.

Selah.

NEVER GIVE UP

Never give up,

Never lose faith.

Hold on to hope.

Trust in God.

He is the Way Maker,

the Miracle Worker,

the Promise Keeper,

the Light in the darkness.

My Jah, that is who You are.

LOVE

Love you will have

Joy you will have

Peace you will have

Strength you will have

Comfort you will have

Healing you will have

Blessing you will have.

I hope you believe in the I AM,

THE MIGHTY YAHWEH.

He will give you this and more,

Even life forevermore. Shalom.

SOME PEOPLE

Some people are mad at you

Because you are not suffering

The way they expect you to.

May God keep on disappointing them.

No matter what may come your way today,

God wants you to know HE'S GOT YOU.

JUST TRUST HIM.

Selah.

TO MY FAMILY AND FRIENDS

To my family and friends

"Let Go" what you cannot change.

Apologize to each other when you should.

Let tears and laughter be your healing medicine

Because tomorrow is not promised to anyone.

May God let love, peace, joy and happiness

Be in our hearts, one towards another now.

HAVE A TERRIFIC DAY.

I LOVE YOU!

Shalom.

Selah.

NEVER

Never give up.

If you fail, fail big, because

F. A. I. L. means "**F**irst **A**ttempt **I**n **L**earning."

The end is not the end, if you have life.

In fact, E. N. D. means "**E**ffort **N**ever **D**ies."

If you get "No" for an answer,

Remember N.O. means "**N**ext **O**pportunity."

So, let's be positive.

PRAYER FOR TODAY

Heavenly Father, ABBA,

I may not understand how everything will work

out, but I trust You.

I don't see a way, but I know You will make a way.

I have faith that at this very moment, You are

touching my heart, opening doors and lining up

the right breaks and opportunities for me.

Things may look dark and bleak, but now, ABBA

Father, You are my light and my way, always in

Jesus name.

Amen. Selah.

IT'S A BEAUTIFUL DAY

It's a beautiful day today.

I just want to thank God for the "Gift of Life."

No REQUESTS, no COMPLAINTS,

Just THANKFUL to be alive,

And make it a happy day, in Jesus name.

Amen.

ABBA

ABBA Father, Thank You for completing what You

started in my life.

I trust that no matter how things seem,

You are my shining light of hope.

I thank You for working behind the scenes

To carry me through to the place of victory

In every area of my life.

YAHSHUA BE PRAISED.

Amen.

Selah.

DECLARE THIS

Today I speak the Word of God over my life and

my circumstances.

I WILL NOT BE DESTROYED!

I WILL NOT BE DEFEATED!

I WILL NOT BE BOUND!

The Lord is my Shepherd, I shall not want.

He lay me down in green pastures and leads me

by still waters.

He restores my soul!

No harm will come near me or my family.

No weapon formed against us shall prosper.

We are covered and kept under the blood of Jesus.

TRAIN

Train your mind to see the good in everything.

Positivity is a choice.

The happiness of your life

Depends on the quality of your thoughts.

Shalom.

NOW

Now may there be peace in your heart,

Love and laughter in your home.

Faith makes all things possible,

Hope makes all things work,

Love makes everything beautiful.

May you have this every day.

Just believe that something amazing is around the

corner,

And it has YOUR name on it.

GOD IS GOOD

God is good all the time.

All the time, God is good.

May God take care of all your needs.

Grant you good health, lasting comfort and

Relief from the burdens of life,

Comfort your soul with gladness and inner peace,

Touch your life with contentment,

Bless your heart with love and faith.

THE BEST

The best kinds of people are the ones who come

into your life and make you see the sun

where you once saw clouds;

The people who believe in you so much that you

start to believe in yourself;

The people who love you simply for being you;

The once in a lifetime kind of people who love you

for who you are.

Selah.

May you

May you find peace and good health,

Not only this day, but for a lifetime,

      in Jesus Holy name, YAHSHUA.

Amen.

HEALTH

Health doesn't come from nutritious food,

  vitamins and medicines alone;

It comes from peace of mind, and

Peace in the heart and soul.

It is magnified by love, laughter, and in ABBA

Father.

Selah.

MIGHTY YAHWEH

Mighty Yahweh be:

Above you to bless you;

Below you to support you;

Before you to guide you;

Behind you to protect you;

Beside you to comfort you; and

Inside you to give you

Strength, love, joy and a lot more.

Amen.

"I AM" IS THE BEAUTY OF LIFE.

WE ALL

We all deserve to always "BELIEVE" that a bit of

"MIRACLE" is waiting for us, somewhere

"NOW!"

JAH KNOW.

Just put love in everything you do.

Start the day with a grateful heart.

Go through your day with

Contentment and positivity.

Have a great day.

Shalom.

Selah.

JAH IS OUR PERFECT GUIDE

Jah is our perfect Guide in life.

His strength overcomes our weaknesses.

His grace fills our emptiness.

His presence overcomes our loneliness.

Walk with Jah every day and never underestimate

the power of your sincere prayers.

Jah bless you.

ABBA FATHER

ABBA Father,

Thank You for the gift of "today."

I choose to focus on the blessing of each moment,

Instead of allowing the little things to steal my joy.

Keep me close to you always,

As I submit every area of my heart and mind to

   You, in Jesus name,

ABBA Father.

EACH MOMENT

Each moment in a day has its own value.

Morning - brings LOVE.

Afternoon - brings HOPE.

Evening - brings FAITH.

Night - brings REST.

I wish you find Jah today, in Jesus name.

Selah.

USE YOUR VOICE

Use your voice for kindness;

Your ears for compassion;

Your hands for charity;

Your mind for truth; and

Your heart for love.

HAVE A NICE DAY.

Selah.

BLESSED

Blessed is the person who understands that the reason for praying is not to have all for yourself but to thank God for all He has given you, so you can help someone else. Amen.

"THIS DAY!"

Good God Almighty.

I kneel down before You at this moment.

Please enlighten what is dark in me,

Strengthen what is weak in me,

The broken pieces in my life, mend them for me,

Heal what is sick in me,

And revive whatever peace and love that has died

     in me.

This is my prayer for me, my family, friends,

     enemies and even those who hate me.

Amen. Selah.

EVERY DAY

Every day with a smile, like a cup of tea,

Warm thoughts in your mind,

Happiness in your soul,

And a heart filled with loving kindness for all.

Have a great day.

WE ARE LIKE

We are like pencils, a ready author,

The best part of us is the inner being,

We make marks as we touch other's lives.

We make mistakes but we become better,

As we are sharpened so we can be on point.

WORRIES

Worries and tensions are like birds,

We cannot stop them from flying near us,

But we can certainly stop them

From making a nest in our mind.

Selah.

WHERE FAITH AND HOPE

Where faith and hope grows, miracles blossom.

May beautiful things happen in your life "now"

When you believe that God is working things out

    for you,

Even if you don't see it or feel it.

God bless you today with miracles and wonders.

Selah.

KEEP GOING

Keep going when you feel like quitting.

Give thanks when you feel like complaining.

Pray when you feel like worrying.

You are very special.

MAY THIS

May this new day be filled with possibilities,

The beginning of a beautiful new start;

As the sun paints the sky in beautiful colours;

As the clouds slowly parts.

IT'S

It's not about who is real to your face,

It's about who stays real behind your back.

DON'T

Don't settle for less.

Jah will power you up when you need it the most.

Dream big.

Believe it.

Achieve it,

It is yours.

MY PRAYER

My prayer for you.

I pray that you would feel confident and

     courageous knowing that your God,

The Alpha and Omega,

The I AM, is fighting for you and working

     everything out for your good.

There is "NOTHING" too big or too difficult for Him

     to do.

Hallelujah.

Selah.

THROUGH LIFE'S JOURNEY

Through life's journey, you get DAMAGED,

DISCOURAGED, and DISTRACTED along the

way.

"DON'T QUIT!"

Believe and agree that "I AM" is with you,

So, get up and start again.

Nothing feels better than knowing that God loves

you.

ALPHA

ALPHA, OMEGA, the I AM is good all the time.

May He bless your heart with love and faith.

Touch your life with contentment,

Grant you good health, lasting comfort and relief

from the burdens of life,

Comfort your soul with gladness and inner peace.

All the time, ALPHA AND OMEGA, I AM is good.

All the time, He is good.

Shalom. Shalom. Shalom.

THINGS

Things have a way of working out.

Never underestimate the power of praying out of

love.

Above all, never underestimate the power of God

Almighty to see you through.

Selah.

EACH DAY I AM

Each day I am thankful for

DREAMS that turned into REALITY;

NIGHT that turned into MORNING;

LIKE that turned into LOVE; and

FRIENDS that turned into FAMILY.

LOVE

Love is never absent in God's eyes.

In God's heart, forgiveness is NEVER impossible.

In God's embrace, no one is ever alone or

forgotten.

ABBA FATHER BLESS YOU

LIFE

Life is a journey with problems,

But Jesus Christ is a Problem Solver.

Lessons to learn but,

Most of all,

We are to enjoy the experiences.

GOOD GOD

Good God,

Please heal the broken people,

Make well the sick,

Restore happiness to those in despair.

Bring love to the lonely,

Food to the hungry and

Peace to the world.

Selah.

Take control of Your children.

WHEN DI ENEMY A PREE YOU

When di enemy a pree you

Just give Jesus Christ the praise,

And dance and confuse dem,

So that God gets the glory,

And you get the victory, in Jesus Name.

Amen.

Selah.

WHEN YOU TURN

When you turn your worries into worship,

The good God Almighty will turn your battles into

blessings.

May the Lord bless you with favour.

Hallelujah.

Selah.

YESTERDAY'S ISSUES

Yesterday's issues;

Don't allow it to trouble your mind.

I refuse to live backwards.

I see every day as a new chapter.

"I Am", the God of Moses, is my inspiration.

AS I

As I walk through this life

That you have given me, Lord,

Thank You that You are the One who guides my

steps.

Selah.

WHEN YOU GIVE

When You Give Jah your weaknesses,

He will give you His strength.

He will stand by us when we are down.

He will encourage us when we think of quitting,

And He will guide us when things seem confusing.

JAH CARES.

I AM!

"I Am," The God of Israel,

Go before you today,

And make a way where there seems to be no way.

May He place the right people in your path,

And move the wrong people out of the way,

So His way is straight before your face.

Selah.

NOW!

Now! Yes, right now!

He who believes in Yahshua, Christ Jesus,

Son of Yahweh,

You are a ready pen to make a mark TODAY!

The mistake of yesterday is behind you,

But TODAY you can make the right decision

To shape your tomorrow or your future,

Only if you believe in YAHSHUA, Christ Jesus,

SON of YAHWEH.

Shalom. Shalom.

BLESSED

Blessed and grateful for another day!

Today, I count my blessings

For the great and small things

He is doing right now;

For the great things

He has in store for me.

For the great things He has done,

I give God the praise.

Hallelujah.

Shalom, Shalom.

DEAR GOD

Dear God,

I just want to thank You for today.

I am smiling,

It's a beautiful day.

I am blessed.

FaTHER GOD

Father God,

I do know that You are my rock and my fortress.

You are my shield and my strong tower.

Help me to anchor myself in You,

And to be strengthened along the way,

In Jesus name I pray.

Amen.

SATURDAY

Saturday, a blessed and wonderful day;

A day to relax,

To be:

Refreshed,

Restored and

Renewed.

Be blessed.

Shalom. Shalom.

SHALOM

Shalom.

The beauty of life does not depend on how happy

you are,

But on how happy others can be because of you.

Shalom.

Shalom.

NOTHING

Nothing makes a new day more beautiful and

      promising than having faith,

The right heart,

The right spirit,

The right mind and

The right strength from Jah.

Selah.

IN JESUS NAME

In Jesus Name,

May you wake up to a beautiful morning,

Filled with peacefulness, love and light.

May you approach the day with

Optimism and hope.

Enjoy yourself and have an awesome day.

Selah.

Amen.

HOW WONDERFUL

How wonderful it is to know

That ABBA Father walks before us, and

Charts crooked places straight.

There is no need to fear the future.

Your steps are ordered by ABBA Father.

Amen.

JaH KNOW

Jah know, a beautiful day is waiting for you.

Run with confidence.

Walk with aims.

Fly with your achievement.

Get up and make this a lovely day.

Selah.

YOUR LIFE

Your life that is in front of you,

Is far more important

Than the life behind you.

Jah know.

Shalom. Shalom.

THE BIBLE

The Bible says we have to

Bless each other so we can live in love.

So, I am writing this message to you.

Today is a day of blessings.

May God bless your heart, your life, your family,

your health, your home, your finances, and

your projects, in the Name of Jesus.

Amen.

GOOD GOD

Good God saw what they did to you.

He felt you dealing with it in silence and hurt.

He saw how they tried to destroy you;

God knows it all.

He kept you and watched over you.

God has prepared a table for you

In the presence of your enemies.

This is your season for blessings and

breakthrough.

Shout "HALLELUJAH" seven times,

In the Name of Jesus.

TIME

Time says, "PLAN ME."

Money says, "EARN ME."

Calendar says, "TURN ME."

Future says, "WIN ME."

Beauty says, "LOVE ME."

But God simply says, "REMEMBER ME."

Selah.

For My presence will always be with you.

THE BLESSINGS

The blessings of this day

Radiates through your smile.

Be helpful with your hands and

Shine through your heart.

God will provide your daily needs,

Only if you believe.

GOOD MORNING

Good morning

A morning is a wonderful blessing,

Whether it is sunny, cloudy, rainy or snowy.

It stands for hope and

Giving us another start in life.

May yours be a great one.

LIFE IS ALWAYS A CHALLENGE

Life is always a challenge, but God sustains us.

Life is hard, but God provides.

Life is unpredictable, but God guides us.

Life is unfair, but God cares for us always.

Shalom. Shalom.

YaHWEH

Yahweh, in Jesus name,

May He lead you now

To where your steps should go,

So that you receive your blessings.

Shalom.

Shalom.

SOMETIMES

Sometimes

God breaks our spirits to save our souls;

God breaks our hearts to make us whole;

God allows pain so we can be stronger;

God sends us failure so we can be humble;

God allowed Jesus Christ to die and raise from the

dead so that we believe in Him;

God allows everything to be taken away from us,

except life, so we can learn the value of

everything He gave us.

Shalom. Shalom.

Selah.

Jamaican Family Talk

My cuz called me and said, "Wah gwaan family?"

I replied, "Mi deh yah. You good?"

Cuz replied, "Yeah man, most things."

I replied, "I ask myself, time and time again, why
good people get the hardest fight in life?
Jah know mi cry."

Cuz said, "A so it set when greatness ah come."

I replied, "Jus like how they did Jesus Christ, and
He is the Alpha and Omega, the beginning
and the end."

Cuz said, "Jah know, same so."

BE HAPPY

Be happy and blessed.

Each new day gives us new reasons to sing God's

praise!

May God bless you abundantly.

May your heart be filled with

songs of praise for Him.

Be blessed.

Selah.

10 THINGS GOD WANTS YOU TO REMEMBER

"I AM" the God of Moses.

I love you.

"I AM" with you.

"I AM" for you.

I will guide you.

I will provide for you.

I will strengthen you.

I will bless you.

I will not fail you.

I will give you rest.

Shalom. Shalom.

WHEN YOU HAVE A LOT OF SETBACKS

When you have a lot of setbacks,

It's because we fail to launch.

An arrow can only be shot

By pulling it backwards.

Be confident and launch forward.

Hallelujah.

Shalom.

Shalom.

WHEN YOU THINK THERE IS NO HOPE

When you think there is no hope,

Jah will say,

"Take My hands and let Me lead the way.

We can do this together.

Be strong and courageous.

Do not be afraid.

I am your Father."

Shalom. Shalom.

LIVE YOUR LIFE

Live your life and be happy.

Yahweh, ABBA Father, did not give you everything

to enjoy life.

Yahweh, ABBA Father, gave you life to enjoy

everything.

Never allow anything to steal your joy and peace.

Shalom. Shalom.

Selah.

Hallelujah.

ABOUT THE AUTHOR

Navern Nelson is a hard-working, dedicated and committed father of two children, who is happily married to his beautiful wife, Jinel. He is a man of faith who looks to God and seeks guidance from the Almighty God, Jesus Christ, in all he does. Navern seeks to inspire individuals as they go through daily hardships and recognize that we must look to Jesus Christ of Nazareth for our daily inspiration.